HAL•LEONARD
INSTRUMENTAL
PLAY-ALONG

AUDIO
ACCESS
INCLUDED

PLAYBACK+
peed • Pitch • Balance • Loop

Billie Eilish

TRUMPET

T0055709

Audio arrangements by Peter Deneff

To access audio, visit:
www.halleonard.com/mylibrary

Enter Code
5235-3241-3475-8841

ISBN 978-1-5400-9211-3

HAL•LEONARD®

Visit Hal Leonard Online at
www.halleonard.com

Contact us:
Hal Leonard
7777 West Bluemound Road
Milwaukee, WI 53213
Email: info@halleonard.com

In Europe, contact:
Hal Leonard Europe Limited
42 Wigmore Street
Marylebone, London, W1U 2RN
Email: info@halleonardeurope.com

In Australia, contact:
Hal Leonard Australia Pty. Ltd.
4 Lentara Court
Cheltenham, Victoria, 3192 Australia
Email: info@halleonard.com.au

CONTENTS

BAD GUY

TRUMPET

Words and Music by BILLIE EILISH O'CONNELL
and FINNEAS O'CONNELL

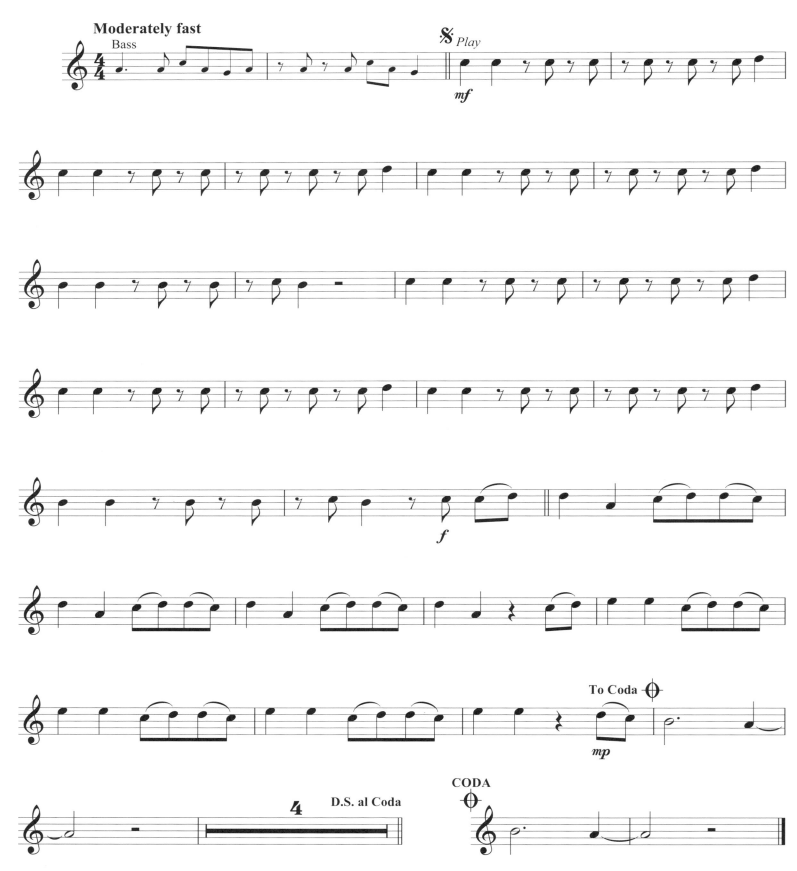

I LOVE YOU

TRUMPET

Words and Music by BILLIE EILISH O'CONNELL
and FINNEAS O'CONNELL

EVERYTHING I WANTED

TRUMPET

Words and Music by BILLIE EILISH O'CONNELL
and FINNEAS O'CONNELL

Idontwannabeyouanymore

TRUMPET

Words and Music by BILLIE EILISH O'CONNELL
and FINNEAS O'CONNELL

LOVELY

TRUMPET

Words and Music by BILLIE EILISH O'CONNELL,
FINNEAS O'CONNELL and KHALID ROBINSON

NO TIME TO DIE

TRUMPET

Words and Music by BILLIE EILISH O'CONNELL
and FINNEAS O'CONNELL

11

OCEAN EYES

TRUMPET

Words and Music by
FINNEAS O'CONNELL

YOU SHOULD SEE ME IN A CROWN

TRUMPET

Words and Music by BILLIE EILISH O'CONNELL
and FINNEAS O'CONNELL

CODA

D.S. al Coda

_mf_

2

_mf_

_f_

1.

2.

WHEN THE PARTY'S OVER

TRUMPET

Words and Music by
FINNEAS O'CONNELL